FR. MARK TOUPS

Advent Meditations
with Mary

ASCENSION

West Chester, Pennsylvania

Nihil obstat: Very Reverend Joshua Rodrigue, STL.
            Censor Librorum
            July 16, 2018

Imprimatur: +Most Reverend Shelton J. Fabre
            Bishop of Houma-Thibodaux
            August 5, 2018

Ascension
Post Office Box 1990
West Chester, PA 19380
1-800-376-0520
ascensionpress.com

Cover design: Faceout Studios
Cover art: Mike Moyers (*The Nativity* ©2018 Mike Moyers, Franklin, TN)
Interior art: Mike Moyers (*The Annunciation, The Visitation, Traveling to Bethlehem, The Manger* ©2018 Mike Moyers, Franklin, TN)
Printed in the United States of America
ISBN 978-1-945179-60-0

CONTENTS

HOW TO USE THIS JOURNAL

Daily Meditations

This journal you have in your hands is an Advent prayer journal with daily meditations. Each week of *Rejoice!* has a theme that allows you to dive deeply into the lessons Mary has to share about welcoming Jesus into her life. Each week's theme will help you walk closer and closer to the ultimate goal of preparing for the person of Jesus, not just preparing for the day of Christmas.

Community

Community is a key component in the journey to holiness. Advent provides a wonderful opportunity to take a little more time to focus on your prayer and grow stronger in friendships on the shared journey to heaven.

The ideal is for a whole parish to take up *Rejoice!* and journey together as a community. You can learn more about how to provide *Rejoice!* to a large parish group at **rejoiceprogram.com,** with information about bulk discounts and parish Advent mission nights with the *Rejoice!* videos.

If you are unable to experience *Rejoice!* as a whole parish, consider a small group setting. Use *Rejoice!* as a family devotion for Advent or get together with a few friends to discuss your prayer and how God is speaking to you in this season.

This doesn't mean you can't use *Rejoice!* as an individual! You can take this journey with Mary through Advent even if you are not meeting in a group or talking about it with friends. You are still not alone – Catholics all over the country are on the same journey you are.

This journal is a place for you to speak to God and to hear and see all that he has to show you.

Videos

To accompany the journal, *Rejoice!* offers videos with Father Mark Toups, Sister Miriam James Heidland, and Father Josh Johnson. Through their witness, conversation, and prayer, you'll find fresh insights into the details of Mary's life and her preparation to welcome Jesus. These are the very same details you'll be praying with through Advent with *Rejoice!*

The program includes a primary *Rejoice!* video and thematic weekly videos. Each Sunday of Advent, you will get access to a quick video from one of the three presenters to energize your reflections and encourage you in your prayer each week. Sign up for these weekly videos at **rejoiceprogram.com** to receive them by email.

FOR YOUR PRAYER

Imaginative Prayer

Each day's reflection will end with a prompt titled "For Your Prayer." There, you will be given a Psalm to pray in preparation, and then a brief Scripture passage to pray with. Here is how to pray with these Scripture passages.

Prepare

Read the passage once. Get familiar with the text, the words, etc. Then slowly read the passage a second time. Pay attention to how you feel as you read. Pay attention to which words strike you.

Next, use your imagination to pray with the passage. In his book *Meditation and Contemplation,* Rev. Tim Gallagher, O.M.V., writes, "In this manner of praying, Saint Ignatius tells us, we imaginatively see the persons in the Bible passage, we hear the words they speak, and we observe the actions they accomplish in the event." So, jump into the Scripture passage. Be in the scene with Mary. Once the scene comes to its natural conclusion, continue with A.R.R.R.

A.R.R.R.

A.R.R.R. is the next step in imaginative prayer. It stands for Acknowledge, Relate, Receive, Respond.

You have sat with God's Word. You have entered into the scene. Now, once you feel God is saying something to you, acknowledge what stirs within you. Pay attention to your thoughts, feelings, and desires. These are important.

After you have acknowledged what's going on inside your heart, relate that to God. Don't just think about your thoughts, feelings, and desires. Don't just think about God or how God might react. Relate to God. Tell him how you feel. Tell him what you think. Tell him what you want. Share all your thoughts, feelings, and desires with God. Share everything with him.

Once you've shared everything with God, receive. Listen to what he's telling you. It could be a subtle voice you hear. It could be a memory that pops up. Maybe he invites you to re-read the Scripture passage. Perhaps he invites you into a still, restful silence. Trust that God is listening to you, and receive what he wants to share with you.

Now, respond. Your response could be more conversation with God. It could be a resolution. It could be tears or laughter. Respond to what you're receiving.

Finally, after picturing the scene with Mary and acknowledging, relating, receiving, and responding, the last step is *journal.* Keep a record this Advent of what your prayer was like. It doesn't have to be lengthy. It could be a sentence or two about what God told you or how the day's reflection struck you. Regardless of how you do it, journaling will help you walk with Mary this Advent. We've provided space in this journal each day for you.

Plan Your Prayer Time with the Five W's

Advent can be a busy season. As you dedicate yourself to prayer this Advent, there is no better safeguard than a good plan. Fr. Josh Johnson, one of the presenters in the *Rejoice!* videos, recommends the Five W's as a method of planning. Here's how it works. Every Sunday, look at your calendar and write out your plan for each of the next six days, answering the following questions: When? Where? What? Who? and Why?

WHEN will I spend time with Jesus?

WHERE will I spend time with Jesus?

WHAT are Jesus and I going to do together?

WHO will hold me accountable to my time with Jesus?

WHY am I prioritizing my time with Jesus?

Having a plan will help you walk with Mary using *Rejoice!* this Advent.

PACE

"The angel Gabriel
was sent from God
to a town of Galilee
called Nazareth."

—Luke 1:26

IN JESUS' DAY

Nazareth was a small village of Galilee in northern Palestine with a population of less than five hundred. To most in Israel, it was a town of little or no importance. In fact, in John 1:46, Nathanael scoffs at the village's insignificance as he asks, "Can anything good come out of Nazareth?"

As an insignificant village tucked away on the outskirts of the Sea of Galilee, not much was happening in Nazareth. It was small. It was poor. It was unassuming. Nazareth escaped the busy hustle and bustle of the big city. The pace of life in Nazareth was much like the pace of life in any small town. Life was simple. The pace was slower.

Mary, born in Nazareth, would have had an inner disposition that reflected the village in which she grew up. Our external environment has a lot to do with our interior environment. The outer pace of Nazareth helped support a contemplative posture within Mary.

The secular Christmas season we find ourselves in is anything but small, simple, and slow. In fact, for many of us, the pace of life accelerates as Christmas nears. There are presents to buy, parties to attend, and holidays to plan.

As the world around us sprints into frenzy, Advent actually invites us to slow down. Just as Nazareth's pace formed the heart of the Mother of God, Mary wants to slow us down so that we can receive as she did. So, slow down. Get quiet. Listen. After all, what's the rush? What are we really preparing for?

For Your Prayer

Mary would have prayed with Psalm 131. Prepare your imaginative prayer by slowly reading Psalm 131. Then, imaginatively pray with Luke 1:26 and ask the Holy Spirit to show you life in Nazareth. Then, pray this prayer:

"Father, regardless of how busy my life is on the outside, I pray that you will help me slow down on the inside."

What words stood out to you as you prayed?
What did you find stirring in your heart?

_____

_____

_____

_____

_____

_____

_____

_____

_____

_____

_____

_____

_____

_____

_____

_____

_____

_____

_____

_____

_____

_____

_____

REJOICE

*"And he came to her and said,
'Hail, full of grace, the
Lord is with you!'"*

—Luke 1:28

THE WORD *ANGEL*

refers to what Gabriel does rather than who Gabriel is. This word derives from the Greek word *aggelos,* which means "messenger." Angels are pure spirits; as such, they have no bodies. Pure spirit is what they are; messenger is what they do. The archangel Gabriel is sent from God to Mary to deliver a message. "And he came to her and said, 'Hail, full of grace, the Lord is with you!'" (Luke 1:28).

The word "hail" in Luke 1:28 may also be translated as "rejoice." The *Ignatius Catholic Study Bible: New Testament* states that the theme of "rejoice" is the lens through which we read the story of Jesus' conception and birth. Gabriel's greeting of "(Rejoice), full of grace" (Luke 1:28) echoes Old Testament passages and signifies that Mary is to be *the* mother of *the* Messiah. Mary, and all of Israel with her, are to "rejoice" because of what God is doing in fulfilling his long-awaited promise. The "rejoicing" is not because of what Mary is doing, but because of what God is doing: "The Lord is with you" (Luke 1:28).

These days leading up to Christmas are different, aren't they? People are usually in a better mood. We smile more. We laugh more. We are more generous. In fact, how often do you hear people say: "I wish it were Christmas all year long?" It is true that at this time of year we tend to "rejoice" a little bit more. However, does true joy stem from the array of holiday decorations or Christmas décor? Our true joy isn't dependent upon the fleeting emotions of December's "Christmas spirit." Those emotions are dependent upon temporary circumstances, but true joy is not.

Mary rejoices because of what God is doing, not because of a holiday season. Mary rejoices in true joy because God is fulfilling his promise.

What about you? What is the source of your "joy" in this holiday season? Is your temperament more influenced by the temporary presence of decorations, décor, and music? Is your happiness in life dependent upon things that seem fragile in their duration? Simply and directly: Are you happy? Are you really happy? What would your life look like if you experienced *true* joy and *real* happiness?

What do you want for Christmas? What do you really want from God this Christmas?

For Your Prayer

Mary would have prayed with Psalm 63. Prepare your imaginative prayer by slowly reading Psalm 63. Then, imaginatively pray with Luke 1:28 and ask the Holy Spirit to show you how Mary lived present to the present moment. Then, pray this prayer:

"Father, take me deeper this Advent. I want this Christmas to be the best Christmas I have ever had. Help me to prepare for Christmas by making this the best Advent I have ever had."

What words stood out to you as you prayed?
What did you find stirring in your heart?

_____

_____

_____

_____

_____

_____

_____

_____

_____

_____

_____

_____

_____

_____

_____

_____

_____

_____

_____

_____

_____

_____

PRESENT

> **"** But she was
> **greatly troubled**
> at the saying. **"**
>
> —Luke 1:29

THOUGH GABRIEL'S

greeting is filled with joy, with all that is meant by the word "rejoice," the Bible reveals an interesting twist to the story. Mary is "greatly *troubled*" at what is said (Luke 1:29). Mary is in awe of the glory of God. She is humbled by Gabriel's power and presence. She experiences anxiety at Gabriel's greeting and questions rise within her heart. However, it is not simply that Mary experiences these emotions, for any of us would likely feel the way Mary feels. It is that Mary is present to the present moment: She is aware of what is stirring in her heart.

There is no evidence that Mary knew that the angel was to meet her in that moment. Chances are, Mary was merely living her life, going about her day as she ordinarily would. However, this day was different, not because of what Mary was doing, but rather because of what God was doing. Mary was simply living her life as she did—present to the present moment. Because of this, she not only recognized the angel's presence, but she heard the greeting from God and was aware of what was stirring within her own heart.

Perhaps the pace of Nazareth helped her to be present. I would imagine that many of us reading this meditation struggle with those two things—that is, living life at a healthy pace and being present to the present moment. Likewise, because of the pace at which we live our lives, far too many of us are not aware of what is really stirring in our hearts. It is there, within us, in our hearts, that we find God waiting for us and God speaking to us. It is deep within us, in our hearts, that we will encounter God.

There is a direct correlation between our pace and our ability to be present to the present moment. And there is a direct connection between living present to the present moment and our ability to be aware of what is stirring within us. The more we live present to the present moment, the more we will be aware of what God is saying to us and how God is leading us. Imagine what your life would look like if you were more aware of what God was saying to you and how God was leading you. Would you want that?

Spend some time today asking yourself: "Am I present to the present moment? Am I *really* present to the people I am with and situations I am dealing with?" Ask Mary for help. Ask her to teach you. Ask her to intercede so that you can be present to the present moment.

For Your Prayer

Mary would have prayed with Psalm 46. Prepare your imaginative prayer by slowly reading Psalm 46. Pray with Luke 1:29 and ask yourself if you are really happy. Then, repeat the prayer we prayed yesterday:

"Father, take me deeper this Advent. I want this Christmas to be the best Christmas I have ever had. Help me to prepare for Christmas by making this the best Advent I have ever had."

What words stood out to you as you prayed?
What did you find stirring in your heart?

_____

_____

_____

_____

_____

_____

_____

_____

_____

_____

_____

_____

_____

_____

_____

_____

_____

_____

_____

_____

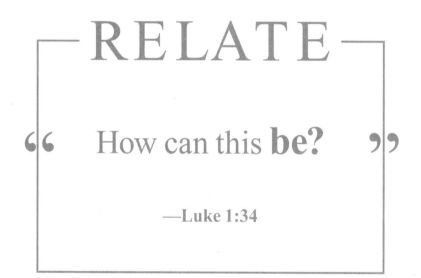

RELATE

" How can this **be?** "

—Luke 1:34

MARY WASN'T THE

only person to speak with an angel. In fact, in the very same chapter of Luke's Gospel, we read that the very same angel also appeared to Zechariah, the father of John the Baptist. Zechariah's response to what God revealed was filled with doubt that God could do such a thing as grant a child to his seventy-year-old wife, Elizabeth. Mary's response in Luke 1:34 was different from Zechariah's doubt in Luke 1:18. Here, Mary was not doubting if God could do such a thing, but merely *how* it would happen.

The clue here is Mary's admission that "I have no husband" (Luke 1:34). According to the *Ignatius Catholic Study Bible: New Testament,* "The Greek text literally reads, 'I do not know man,' which refers to Mary's virginal status rather than her marital status. Her concern is not that she is unmarried but that she is a virgin at present and that she intends to remain one in the future. The announcement of a miraculous conception thus causes Mary to wonder aloud how God will bless her with a son and still honor her vow to perpetual virginity."

Mary knows God. She knows with whom she is speaking. Instead of just thinking about her question, Mary *relates* her thoughts to God. There is a difference between thinking about God and talking with God. In its purest definition, prayer is relating to God. Devotion, adoration, and intercession are time-honored; however, if we are going to develop a relationship with God, then we need to relate to God. Of course, if we are going to relate to God, we have to be aware of what is really going on in our hearts.

To the degree that we are aware of what is stirring within us, we are able to then relate those things to God. So, there is a connection between living present to the present moment and being aware of what is really happening within us and so knowing what to relate to God in prayer.

What do you need to talk to God about? What thoughts, feelings, or desires do you need to share with him? Spend some time with Mary. Ask her to teach you how to relate everything to God.

For Your Prayer

Mary would have prayed with Psalm 42. Prepare your imaginative prayer by slowly reading Psalm 42. Use your spiritual senses and imaginatively pray with Mary in Luke 1:34. Then, pray this prayer:

"Father, I beg you to loosen my thoughts, feelings, and desires so that I share all things with you."

What words stood out to you as you prayed?
What did you find stirring in your heart?

_____

_____

_____

_____

_____

_____

_____

_____

_____

_____

_____

_____

_____

_____

_____

_____

_____

_____

_____

_____

_____

_____

TRUST

> ## "Do not be afraid."
>
> —Luke 1:30

AS GOD'S MESSENGER,

the angel Gabriel senses that Mary is "greatly troubled at the saying." So Gabriel immediately responds, "Do not be afraid." Similar words spoken to Abram in Genesis 15:1 invited the father of the Israelites into a covenant of trust. Identical words to the young Daniel in Daniel 10:12 invited him to trust that God would free his people from bondage. When God's chosen are "greatly troubled," God's invitation is to trust.

Mary is invited to trust ... and imagine all that she had to be afraid of. Who was she, after all, to be worthy of being chosen? Throughout the next few months, she would need to trust God. When she told her parents, she had to trust. When she told Joseph, she had to trust. When the gossipers of small-town Nazareth whispered, she had to trust. During the emotional roller coaster imbuing her pregnancy, Mary had to trust God with all of her fears.

Each of us knows fear. In fact, if you want to find fear, follow the trail of restlessness, worry, and anxiety. What do you worry about? Where is your anxiety? When do you get restless? Underneath those ordinary emotions is fear—and where there is fear, there is God waiting for us to trust him. Perhaps this is one of the reasons we live life at the pace we do. Believe it or not, living busily, or at least living too busily, can be a hidden way that we run from our interior life. Our pace can prevent us from slowing down enough to become aware of those things that stir within. If deep within our hearts we carry restlessness, worry, and anxiety, we can run from that fear by living busily on the outside, so as to avoid facing things on the inside.

One of the things that prevents us from paying attention to what is within is the fear that we are alone. In 1 John 4:18, we are reminded that "perfect love casts out fear." We are not alone; each of us is important to God, who is perfect love. No matter what is going on in your life right now, the antidote for fear is not courage but trust.

Spend some time with Mary today. Ask her if she was afraid. Ask her how she dealt with it. Ask her to help you trust her Son.

For Your Prayer

Mary would have prayed with Psalm 37. Prepare your imaginative prayer by slowly reading Psalm 37:1-11. Use your spiritual senses and imaginatively pray with Mary in Luke 1:30. Then, pray this prayer:

"Father, I ask for the grace today to receive your perfect love that casts out all fear. I beg you to help me trust you in all things."

What words stood out to you as you prayed?
What did you find stirring in your heart?

_____

_____

_____

_____

_____

_____

_____

_____

_____

_____

_____

_____

_____

_____

_____

_____

_____

_____

_____

_____

_____

_____

CONTROL

"May it be done to me."

—Luke 1:38

MARY FREELY AND

actively embraces God and his invitation. Her exultant "may it be done to me according to your word" (Luke 1:38 NAB) is more than a simple acceptance. The literal meaning of the original Greek text indicates that she actually longs for what God is asking. Mary knows the Lord. She trusts God, not because of what he asks but because of who is asking.

Luke 1:38 tells us just as much about Mary as it does about God. Every day preceding the Annunciation Mary lived as if God was really in control of her life. Mary said "yes" every day. Mary's "yes" was birthed out of her "no." Mary was not in control of her life. She said "no" to living life on her terms. She said "no" to "being her own woman." She said "no" to control, for she knew it to be an illusion.

Control is like chasing tomorrow—once you think you are almost there, it slips ahead of you. None of us is truly in control of our life, but the illusion that we are is in the air we breathe. The more we grasp for control, the more tiresome life becomes. Grasping at control, whether it be to control people or circumstances, usually leads to unmet expectations. Unmet expectations, especially those we project onto God, undermine trust in him and trap us in self-sufficiency.

Where are you trying to control your life? What issues, relationships, or dreams are you trying to control? Do your daily actions reflect control or trust? _____

Spend some time with Mary today. Ask her to show you how she lived her daily life before the Annunciation. Ask her to show you how she lived out of control. Ask her to help you live the same way.

For Your Prayer

Mary would have prayed with Psalm 62. Prepare your imaginative prayer by slowly reading Psalm 62. Use your spiritual senses and imaginatively pray with Mary in Luke 1:26-38. Then, pray this prayer:

"Father, I want to experience your presence in such a deeply personal way that I would be free to willingly surrender control of my life to you."

What words stood out to you as you prayed?
What did you find stirring in your heart?

_____
_____
_____
_____
_____
_____
_____
_____
_____
_____
_____
_____
_____
_____
_____
_____
_____
_____
_____
_____
_____
_____
_____

EMPTY

"To a virgin betrothed."

—Luke 1:27

IN HER CLASSIC

contemplation on Mary entitled *The Reed of God,* Caryll Houselander writes, "That virginal quality, for want of a better word, I call emptiness." Mary's virginity can be more personally understood through her profound emptiness.

Numbers 30:4-6 outlines prescriptions for a Jewish woman vowed to perpetual virginity and complete consecration to the Lord. Steeped in biblical wisdom, the early Church Fathers wrote that Mary vowed such Old Testament consecration, embracing the fullness of biblical virginity. In other words, Mary had long intended to remain a virgin and had made such a promise to God before and after the betrothal.

Mary's virginity points us to her emptiness. She was empty of anything that was not of God. She was empty of anything that would prevent her from resting in her deep union with the Father. Yes, she was empty, but her emptiness was not the same as lacking something. Her emptiness came from her deep union, a union so important to her that she had made a vow of virginity even as a married woman.

Many of us panic at the sheer thought of emptiness. A subtly compulsive need to always have something fill us is an epidemic fed by the pace at which we live. We are encouraged to fill our lives with more and more so that we will not have to face our fear of emptiness. The emptiness and freedom within Mary is an invitation to us.

What needs to be emptied from our lives? What are we filling our lives with, yet remaining unfulfilled in the end?

Spend some time with Mary, and ask her what needs emptying so that you might receive as she did.

For Your Prayer

Mary would have prayed with Psalm 63. Prepare your imaginative prayer by once again praying with Psalm 63. Then, imaginatively pray with Luke 1:27 and ask the Holy Spirit to show you Mary in Nazareth.

"Father, I ask for the grace today to empty my heart of anything that is not of you."

What words stood out to you as you prayed?
What did you find stirring in your heart?

_____
_____
_____
_____
_____
_____
_____
_____
_____
_____
_____
_____
_____
_____
_____
_____
_____
_____
_____
_____
_____
_____

The Second Week of Advent

Judea

ECHO

> *"My soul*
>
> *magnifies the*
>
> **LORD."**

—Luke 1:26

AFTER THE ANGEL

departs from her, Mary soon goes "with haste" to a town in Judah (see Luke 1:39). Her pilgrimage south to Judah brings her to the home of her cousin Elizabeth. Immediately upon arrival, Mary receives Elizabeth's greeting and then responds with the first chords of her great Magnificat: "My soul magnifies the Lord" (Luke 1:46).

We know that as the Mother of God, Mary was a unique person. However, how can a human magnify that which is greater? Fr. Scott Traynor helps us understand how Mary's soul magnifies God with the image of Echo Canyon, Colorado. Echo Canyon has breathtaking postcard views around every corner. However, it is not only famous for its scenery. If you stand at the right spot and shout out your name, the sound will reverberate throughout the entire canyon, echoing over and over and ascending louder and louder. Echo Canyon, because it has been perfectly designed to do so, receives a spoken word and perfectly magnifies it for the world to hear. So Echo Canyon is not greater than your voice, nor can it generate anything on its own. Because it is perfectly shaped, however, the canyon magnifies your voice for the world to hear.

Mary does magnify the Lord. Mary's soul, like Echo Canyon, perfectly receives God and echoes to the world what she hears. Remember her *emptiness?* It makes for perfect *echo.*

In a sense, we too are Echo Canyon. Our souls were made to magnify God and echo his glory for the world to hear. However, our souls (the canyon) are wounded, cluttered, and out of tune, so we often don't echo what God says. We will echo something else entirely different.

How is your echo? How empty is your soul from anything that would prevent perfect reverberation of the divine Word? What needs to be emptied from your life so that your soul can echo as Mary's did?

For Your Prayer

Mary would have prayed with the first book of Samuel. Prepare your imaginative prayer by slowly reading 1 Samuel 2:1-10. Use your spiritual senses and imaginatively pray with Mary in Luke 1:46. Then, pray this prayer:

"Father, I ask for the grace of perfect echo. I beg you to reveal anything that prevents my soul from magnifying your voice."

What words stood out to you as you prayed?
What did you find stirring in your heart?

_____

_____

_____

_____

_____

_____

_____

_____

_____

_____

_____

_____

_____

_____

_____

_____

_____

_____

_____

_____

_____

Second Week — SUNDAY

CERTAIN

"Blessed is she who
believed."

—Luke 1:45

SCRIPTURE STUDY

helps us understand the miracle of Elizabeth's conceiving. She was likely more than seventy years old. When Gabriel promised that Elizabeth was with child, Mary believed. As she set out in haste for Judah, Mary was certain that Elizabeth was pregnant. Mary was certain that she herself was pregnant. When Mary left Nazareth for Judah, she had no physical evidence. She could not see physical signs of her own pregnancy, nor could she even see Elizabeth. But Mary was certain.

Once in Judah, Elizabeth greets Mary with rejoicing and proclaims her blessed, for "blessed is she who believed that there would be a fulfilment of what was spoken to her from the Lord" (Luke 1:45). The Greek expression translated as "believed" denotes a certainty, an unquestioning conviction that has no need for physical evidence. God said it, and Mary believed it. She was certain it would come to be. Mary's certainty was not what she could see before her; it was from the one who promised. Mary is certain, not because of what God did, but because it was God who said it would be done.

Many of us have often asked God for help. Once we ask, however, the answer may not come in our time frame. The more that time passes and our prayer appears to be unfulfilled, doubt enters our mind. We wonder, "Did God really hear me?" Or, we think, "Is God going to come through on his promise?" In Habakkuk 2:3, God reminds us that his promise "awaits its time; it hastens to the end—it will not lie. If it seem slow, wait for it; it will surely come, it will not delay." In other words, if God makes a promise, it is a promise, although it might not unfold as quickly as we would like. We need to believe that God is faithful to his word. In fact, we should be certain.

Have you asked God for help recently? If so, how did God respond? What did God say in reply? Even if you are still waiting for the results, be patient and be certain that what he promised will come to be. As you wait, wait with Mary. Spend some time with her today and wait together.

Mary rejoices because of what God is doing, not because of a holiday season. Mary rejoices in true joy because God is fulfilling his promise.

For Your Prayer

Mary would have prayed with the book of Isaiah. Prepare your imaginative prayer by slowly reading Isaiah 55. Use your spiritual senses and imaginatively pray with Mary in Luke 1:45. Then, pray this prayer:

"Father, I ask to know how personal your promises are for me. I beg you to reveal how you have always come through on your promises."

What words stood out to you as you prayed?
What did you find stirring in your heart?

_____

_____

_____

_____

_____

_____

_____

_____

_____

_____

_____

_____

_____

_____

_____

_____

_____

_____

_____

_____

STRUGGLE

" He has regarded
the low estate
of his handmaiden.**"**

—Luke 1:48

ON SUNDAY WE SAW

how Mary's emptiness fostered her echo. Today we hear Mary glorifying God in her lowliness, and there is no coincidence. Emptiness leads to echo ... and struggle leads to emptiness. The Greek word Mary uses to describe her lowliness is the word *tapeinosin,* which describes not simply a spiritual humility but a condition of great suffering. In fact, the word was commonly used in the Septuagint, the Greek version of the Old Testament, to depict the affliction of God's people when they were persecuted and oppressed but about to be rescued by God's saving hand. For example, recalling how God once freed Israel from its slavery in Egypt, Psalm 136 says, "It is he who remembered us in our low estate *(tapeinosin)* ... and rescued us from our foes."

As a Jewish woman living during the affliction of Roman occupation, Mary would have lived in the daily cry from a suffering people. The village of Nazareth and the people of Israel yearned for God to save them from their suffering.

Struggles, even suffering, are a reality for many of us. While dismissed by our culture, struggles pervade the lives of everyone. Few of us embrace our struggles, yet all of us face them. Struggle is a part of life. Furthermore, there is a lie whispered deep within our struggles that says, "I'm alone." Thus, many of us run from struggles and suffering because we fear abandonment more than we fear the struggle—none of us wants to struggle alone.

It is important for us to know that struggles and suffering are not a consequence of God abandoning us. Struggle is a part of life. In fact, Mary sings of her lowliness *(tapeinosin)* because she knows she is not alone. God has chosen her, so she need not run from suffering. She can remain empty, for God "has regarded the low estate of his handmaiden."

Where in your life are you struggling? More importantly, what is your attitude toward struggles and suffering? Toward your own struggle? Toward others' struggles? Ask Mary how she dealt with struggles and suffering.

For Your Prayer

Mary would have prayed with Psalm 22. Prepare your imaginative prayer by slowly reading Psalm 22:1-8; 19-31. Use your spiritual senses and imaginatively pray with Mary in Luke 1:48. Then, pray this prayer:

"Father, I ask to know your love for me in my weakness. Help me not to run away from suffering, but to run to you in the suffering."

What words stood out to you as you prayed?
What did you find stirring in your heart?

_____

TURN

" **Mary** ... returned to her home. "

—Luke 1:56

THE GOSPEL OF LUKE

tells us that "Mary remained with … [Elizabeth] about three months, and returned to her home" (Luke 1:56). As Mary began the nine-day pilgrimage from Judah back to Nazareth, her trip was paved with the unknown. Mary was a young pregnant teenager in a Jewish culture that handled such situations by stoning. Mary knew Elizabeth's reassurance, but she also knew the reality of Mosaic Law and the judgment of small-town Nazareth. Furthermore, it is very likely that Mary was returning to her home town with her relatives. Certainly, they noticed she was beginning to show physical signs of pregnancy, and in the awkward silence of isolation, one can imagine how fear whispered to Mary as she "returned to her home." Through it all, Mary had to turn to God.

When she returned home, she immediately returned to Joseph. Since the Scriptures say that Mary "went with haste," we can presume that she left Nazareth for Judah before she had a chance to speak with Joseph (see Luke 1:39). Remember, unlike modern Western tradition, betrothal in Jewish culture at the time was more than simple engagement. Betrothal was a temporary period, which could last up to a year, between the celebration of the marriage covenant and when the spouses would begin living together under the same roof.

Joseph and Mary had already entered into the covenant of marriage. During this betrothal period, Joseph was preparing their home and preparing for Mary to move in. While Mary was readying herself in Judah, Joseph was in Galilee preparing for her return. However, her return brought more than he was prepared for. When Joseph found his bride "she was found to be with child" (Matthew 1:18).

Imagine the look on Joseph's face when he first saw Mary's pregnant body. Imagine his shock at the explanation that it was "of the Holy Spirit." Likewise, imagine Mary and her emotional reaction to Joseph's response. As Joseph "resolved to send her away quietly," Mary once again had to turn to God.

When we encounter suffering, the temptation is for us to turn in on ourselves rather than turning to God. A decision of the will is required if we are going to stay in a receptive relationship with God. However, as we wait for the Lord, we might grow tired of waiting, grow tired of the struggle. The temptation is to attempt to fix the problem rather than stay focused on the Lord and trust in his response.

In her struggles, Mary makes a decision of the will. She turns to God and decides to receive. When you struggle, where do you turn? Do you turn to the Lord, and, if so, for how long? Do you turn inward and try to fix it? Do you turn to vice and try to forget?

For Your Prayer

Mary would have prayed with Psalm 23. Prepare your imaginative prayer by slowly reading Psalm 23. Use your spiritual senses and imaginatively pray with Mary in Luke 1:56. Then, pray this prayer:

"Father, even when I am in my dark valley, help me to turn to you and know that you are at my side."

What words stood out to you as you prayed? What did you find stirring in your heart?

_____

_____

_____

_____

_____

_____

_____

_____

_____

_____

_____

_____

_____

_____

_____

_____

_____

_____

_____

_____

_____

WAIT

"All this took place."

—Matthew 1:22

AS JOSEPH SIFTED

through his decision to divorce Mary quietly, we often forget how long Mary may have had to wait for Joseph to change his mind. What was Mary doing while "all this took place?" Mary waited. With her heart turned towards God—with her spirit empty yet aware of her struggle—Mary waited.

While Mary waited, she remained in relationship with God. She disclosed her thoughts to him. She related her feelings. She shared her desires. While Mary waited for Joseph, she waited with God—and there was much happening in the waiting.

Most of us don't like to wait. Television commercials are littered with gadgets and gizmos that save us time so that we don't have to wait. For most of us, waiting means the delay of what we want. However, Mary embraced the waiting because Mary waited with God.

Most of us long to be in control. We have our own plans for our life. Earlier in the week, we read in Habakkuk 2:3 that God's plan "hastens to the end—it will not lie. If it seems slow, wait for it; it will surely come, it will not delay." There is a difference between waiting for God to do something versus waiting with God as he does something. When we wait *for* God to do what we have asked him, then the wait can seem empty. However, when we wait *with* God as he does something, then the waiting is filled with intimacy and union.

Have you asked God to do something in your life? If so, are you still waiting? Spend some time with Mary and ask her to describe her waiting.

For Your Prayer

Mary would have prayed with Psalm 27. Prepare your imaginative prayer by slowly reading Psalm 27. Use your spiritual senses and imaginatively pray with Mary as she waited in Matthew 1:22. Then, pray this prayer:

"Father, I ask for the grace today to taste your personal love for me. I beg you to help me wait with you while you do great things in my life."

What words stood out to you as you prayed?
What did you find stirring in your heart?

_____

_____

_____

_____

_____

_____

_____

_____

_____

_____

_____

_____

_____

_____

_____

_____

_____

_____

_____

_____

VULNERABLE

> "You discern my thoughts."
>
> —Psalm 139:2

WHEN THE ANGEL

Gabriel greets Mary with "rejoice," few of us would imagine that the reality of struggle and waiting would be a part of her rejoicing. However, isn't that exactly what many of us are challenged with? There are few other times in the year when we are invited to look this deeply within our hearts. The stretch from Thanksgiving to Christmas invites us to rejoice in gratitude, family, and the Incarnation. However, for many of us, this time of year can feel vulnerable.

The struggles of life tend to get amplified during Advent. What is good in our life or marriage or family tends to feel even better. But what is messy in our life or marriage or family also tends to get amplified or magnified.

The holidays place different pressures on us. Decisions have to be made—travel plans, family preparations, and finances all come up. If this weren't enough, holidays with children introduce a new variety of parenting needs which can play on the agreements or disagreements couples have in their parenting philosophy. Then throw in your in-laws, your siblings, and your extended family. Everyone seems to have opinions to express and desires to plan around.

Simply put, perhaps no other time of the year leaves us feeling more vulnerable than the holidays. A lot of us want to run from vulnerability. Either we run away, pretending all is well, or we run into an over-busy, frenetic pace during the holidays, trying to over-manage the struggle within. Perhaps the question is not whether or not we feel vulnerable, but where to turn in our vulnerability.

Mary felt the vulnerability of waiting as she waited for Joseph. Mary can teach us what to do if we allow her heart to speak to our heart. Remember, Mary stayed in relationship with God. She remembered what God had done in the past as an anchor for trusting him in the present moment. Furthermore, Mary didn't ruminate in her fear or anxiety. Instead she shared everything in her heart with God. She related everything. Because she knew who she was talking to, she was able to let go of control so that she was more able to receive from God.

Be not afraid. Be honest about life, but be not afraid in the midst of it all. Spend some time with Mary and ask her to teach you what to do in vulnerability.

For Your Prayer

Mary would have prayed with Psalm 139. Prepare your imaginative prayer by slowly reading Psalm 139:1-16. Then, pray this prayer:

"Father, I ask for the grace today to taste your personal love for me. I beg you to help me wait with you in my vulnerability."

What words stood out to you as you prayed? What did you find stirring in your heart?

_____

_____

_____

_____

_____

_____

_____

_____

_____

_____

_____

_____

_____

_____

_____

_____

_____

_____

_____

_____

PROMISES

"As the angel of the Lord commanded."

—Matthew 1:24

WHILE MARY

continued to wait, the angel Gabriel returned to the Advent story, this time visiting Joseph. Encouraged with God's initiative, Joseph submitted to God's plan. Joseph reversed his previous decision to divorce Mary and "did as the angel of the Lord commanded him; he took his wife" (Matthew 1:24). Imagine how this news would have affected Mary, for once again God had come through on his promise.

God promised her that she would miraculously conceive the Son of God. God promised her that Elizabeth had conceived in her old age. Throughout the Advent story, we see the good news of God's initiative. Here we see the good news of God's heart: When God makes a promise, God always comes through on his promise.

The Bible is filled with the story of God's promises—to Abraham, Sarah, and Isaac; to Moses; to David; to Elijah; to Israel, promising return from exile; and to others. Throughout salvation history, God makes promises of his fidelity. Each time, with each situation, God comes through on his promise.

While you may still be waiting—and while you may still feel the vulnerability of waiting—it is important to remember not merely what God has promised but that it is he who made the promise. God can be trusted. His fidelity, especially as revealed in the Advent story, reminds us that he always comes through on his promise.

Take some time today to remember. Look back on your life. While the promises may have been fulfilled differently from the way you would have wanted, look back on God's coming through on his promises in your life. What has God done for you? How has he fulfilled his promises?

For Your Prayer

Mary would have prayed with Psalm 136. Prepare your imaginative prayer by slowly reading Psalm 136. Use your spiritual senses and imaginatively pray with Mary as she waited in Matthew 1:24. Then, pray this prayer:

"Father, I ask for the grace today to remember all that you have done for me. Strengthen my trust in what you will do because of my remembrance of what you have done already."

What words stood out to you as you prayed? What did you find stirring in your heart?

_____

_____

_____

_____

_____

_____

_____

_____

_____

_____

_____

_____

_____

_____

_____

_____

_____

_____

_____

_____

_____

_____

_____

The Third Week of Advent

Journey

PLANS

"A decree went out from Caesar Augustus that all the world should be enrolled."

—Luke 2:1

THE ADVENT STORY

deepens as soon as news of a census descends upon Nazareth. Just when Mary and Joseph are adjusting to the fullness of married life, the emperor of Rome decrees a census. Mary and Joseph must deal with this unexpected demand. Once again, Mary must face a chapter in life that was not in her plans.

Mary wasn't expecting Gabriel's annunciation. She wasn't expecting Joseph's initial response to divorce her. She certainly wasn't expecting having to travel at eight-and-a-half months pregnant. Going to Bethlehem was not in her plans. In fact, none of this was in her plans. Mary likely had plans about what her life and marriage would look like, but that all changed. Adapting well, Mary made new plans for what her pregnancy and birth would be like, and now that too has changed. Now here comes the call for the enrollment and yet another new set of plans.

Each of us has our plans. Each of us has our idea or dream or image of how we want our life to unfold. However, our plans seldom unfold according to how we think they should. In fact, often when we evaluate our lives, we realize that life is different from what we expected—our plans rarely come to pass. Whether or not your life has unfolded according to your plans, trust that God knows his plans.

It is important for us to realize God does indeed have a plan for each of our lives. However, we often try to be in control. We have our expectations; we have our plans. This limits God's ability to navigate in our lives. Mary teaches us how to give room to God for what he wants to unfold.

God's plans for us are more akin to dancing than destination. In other words, God's ultimate plan for us is for us to live with him forever in heaven. His ultimate plan for us is to experience the joy, freedom, and happiness for which he created us. However, in the midst of the journey of life, his plan unfolds one day at a time. Like a couple dancing in the joy of the song, the lead partner is always watching what the other is doing in the dance. A good lead dancer responds to how the other moved. Based off of how she moved, the leader responds anew and then waits to see how the dance unfolds.

God's plans for us are constantly adapting to where we are in life and how we ourselves have responded to his latest prompting. All of what is in his heart is only for our best: for our joy, freedom, and happiness. Spend some time today with Mary and ask her about God's plans for your life.

For Your Prayer

Mary would have prayed with the book of Jeremiah. Prepare your imaginative prayer by slowly reading Jeremiah 29:11-14. Use your spiritual senses and imaginatively pray with Mary in Luke 2:1. Then, pray this prayer:

"Father, I ask for the grace today to taste your love for me and my life. I beg you to help me trust you and to trust your plans for my life."

What words stood out to you as you prayed?
What did you find stirring in your heart?

_____

_____

_____

_____

_____

_____

_____

_____

_____

_____

_____

_____

_____

_____

_____

_____

_____

_____

_____

_____

ORDINARY

"Mary ... was
with child."

—Luke 2:5

MARY WOULD HAVE

had quite a ninety-mile pilgrimage to Bethlehem. Mary was "with child," and traveling on a donkey would probably have caused her some discomfort. Without a chair to support her lower back, the constant swaying from the donkey's rhythm intensified her discomfort. Given how far along she was in her pregnancy, Mary probably had less energy and craved more rest.

Because of the long journey, however, Mary couldn't get the rest she desired. Mary's journey was anything but easy. She probably experienced similar discomfort to any other pregnant woman on such a journey. Yet Mary "was with child," and she knew who that child was. Throughout her journey, especially when her discomfort intensified, she placed her hands on her womb and was reminded that God was with her. Her discomfort may have been like the discomfort of any ordinary pregnancy; however, Mary knew God is in the ordinary.

Most of our life is ordinary, even during this special time of year. We sit in traffic. We wait in long lines at department stores. We clean our house for the holidays. Most of life is not flashy; it is just rather ordinary. Furthermore, many of us struggle to find God with us in the ordinary. Imagine for a moment that if God really is with you in the midst of everything, just how much God wants to be with you in the midst of all of the ordinary details of life. The truth is that God is with you—twenty-four hours a day, seven days a week. Yes, God is with you, even in the ordinary.

Take some time and ask Mary to describe the ordinary truths of her trip to Bethlehem. How do you feel about your ordinary life? Do you see a connection between your ordinary life and your spiritual life?

Mary rejoices because of what God is doing, not because of a holiday season. Mary rejoices in true joy because God is fulfilling his promise.

For Your Prayer

Mary would have prayed with Psalm 100. Prepare your imaginative prayer by slowly reading Psalm 100. Use your spiritual senses and imaginatively pray with Mary in Luke 2:5. Then, pray this prayer:

"Father, I long to taste your presence in my ordinary life. I beg you to open my heart so that I may do all things, even ordinary things, with you."

What words stood out to you as you prayed?
What did you find stirring in your heart?

EVERYTHING

"All went to be enrolled,
each to his own city."

—Luke 2:3

THE DECREE DID NOT

simply affect Mary and Joseph; it affected everyone, for "all went to be enrolled." The news of the census sent shock waves throughout all of Galilee. Nazareth would have quickly frenzied as every anxious pilgrim hastily prepared to journey "to his own city."

Once again, Mary found herself filled with questions. When was her baby due? How long would it take to get to Bethlehem? Would they make it to Bethlehem in time? Joseph, too, had questions. Could Mary's body handle the journey? Where would they stay once they arrived? Would his meager savings be enough for the census tax plus the journey there and back? The census didn't simply present a convenient fulfillment for the prophet Micah's messianic prophecy (see Micah 5:2), it presented Mary and Joseph with penetrating questions demanding further trust and absolute dependency. The journey to Bethlehem demanded everything.

Sometimes, divine intimacy calls us to places we don't want to go. Sometimes we wonder, "God, I've given you so much already; do you want everything?"

The answer is … yes, God does want everything. But, remember, God seeks intimacy. If the essentials for intimacy are complete self-donation and unbridled receptivity, then this is a two-way street. If God requires your complete self-donation, then he is prepared to give you himself. If God requires unbridled receptivity, then he desires to receive all of you. God requires everything so that he can give us everything. The stretching we feel "in the everything" is so that we are more able to receive everything he wants to give us.

Spend some time with Mary. Ask her how she surrendered everything.

For Your Prayer

Mary would have prayed with the book of Genesis. Prepare your imaginative prayer by slowly reading Genesis 22:1-19. Use your spiritual senses and imaginatively pray with Mary in Luke 2:3. Then, pray this prayer:

"Father, I desire to taste just how much you want me. I give you permission to lead me wherever you want so that I may give you everything."

What words stood out to you as you prayed?
What did you find stirring in your heart?

_____

_____

_____

_____

_____

_____

_____

_____

_____

_____

_____

_____

_____

_____

_____

_____

_____

_____

_____

_____

_____

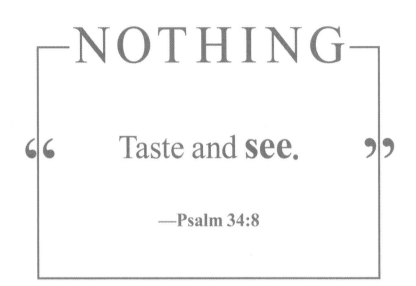

NOTHING

"

Taste and **see.**

"

—Psalm 34:8

IN ANCIENT TIMES,

the ninety-mile trip from Nazareth to Bethlehem would have taken about a week and a half. As each day fades and tomorrow turns into today, Mary and Joseph have less and less to give. Soon, it feels they have *nothing* left to give.

Often, when you have given everything, you may feel as if you have *nothing* left to give. You might feel this way when you have fought hard to nurture your marriage, only to feel like you are the only one fighting for it. You may feel this way with broken relationships, as if you are the only one who has worked hard for reconciliation and forgiveness. You can feel this way with people, with circumstances, and even with life.

Many of us at this time of year may feel as if we have nothing left to give, perhaps even with the very people we will see at holiday gatherings. This time of year may bring us into contact with people we only see once a year. For some of these people, it doesn't take long for us to remember why we only see them once a year. We may have tried and tried and have nothing left to give.

The question is: What do we do when we have nothing left to give? God may have asked us to give everything. When we have nothing left to give, what do we do? There, when we have nothing left to give, our only response is to surrender. Yesterday, we prayed with the reality that we may be required to give everything. Today, we acknowledge that doing so may make us feel as if we have nothing left to give. It is there that we discover the truth of who God is. God is always with us. ⎯⎯⎯⎯⎯

What Mary teaches us during Advent is how to receive. She received God in the Annunciation, so much so that she actually conceived God in her womb! Mary teaches us how to live; she teaches us how to receive from God.

God is forever wanting to lead us, to bless us, to pour his love into us. When we have given everything, we are more disposed to receive everything from him. When we have nothing left to give, there is often nothing left to prevent us from receiving him.

When you feel as if you have nothing left to give, stop trying. Stop trying to give what you don't have. Let God give it *through* you; let God give it to you. When you have nothing left to give in your marriage or in your family or in broken relationships, God can give you what you need, giving those relationships what they need through your receptivity.

Spend some time today with Mary and ask her to reveal to you how God blessed her when she had nothing left to give.

For Your Prayer

Mary would have prayed with Psalm 34. Prepare your imaginative prayer by slowly reading Psalm 34. Use your spiritual senses and imaginatively pray with Mary in Luke 2:3. Then, pray this prayer:

"Father, I desire to taste just how much you want me. I give you permission to lead me wherever you want so that I may give you everything."

What words stood out to you as you prayed?
What did you find stirring in your heart?

_____

_____

_____

_____

_____

_____

_____

_____

_____

_____

_____

_____

_____

_____

_____

_____

_____

_____

_____

_____

_____

POVERTY

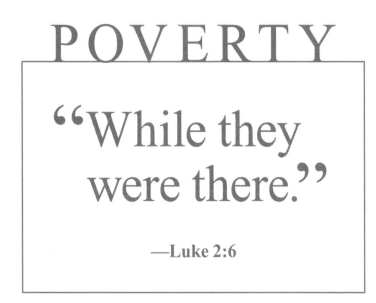

"While they were there."

—Luke 2:6

AS MARY AND JOSEPH

arrive in Bethlehem, the calm silence of their journey is invaded by the frantic noise of thousands of pilgrims cramming into the city for the census. Joseph's meager income had not provided for the emperor's surprise decree, so the simplicity of his Galilean lifestyle was strained. There was the census tax. There were the travel expenses. Mary and Joseph had not prepared for any of this. Plus, it was a seller's market, and the unexpected census created an unseasonable demand. Everything cost more—food, water, lodging, etc. This young couple, tired from ninety miles of exhausting travel, had no one and nothing. They were utterly dependent on God in their poverty.

God is not afraid of our being dependent upon him; he is not afraid of our poverty. After all, it was the canvas upon which he painted his birth into humanity. Many of us, though, run from dependency. Many of us run from our inner poverty. Perhaps this is because it feels like we are dying: as we let go, it feels as if we have nothing to hold on to. Perhaps it is because we feel vulnerable, and vulnerability feeds panic because it means a loss of security. Perhaps it is because we have nothing to offer God—and we really believe that we have to give God something in order for him to love us. Perhaps it is because we are afraid that "I'm alone, and God won't come through."

Now, listen to the voice of God: "Blessed are the poor in spirit, for theirs is the kingdom of heaven" (Matthew 5:3). God loves the poor. Why? As we have learned from Mary in our previous meditations, poverty leads to emptiness ... emptiness leads to a perfect echo ... and echo leads to perfect worship.

Mary was empty, which means she was poor. Spend some time with Mary and ask her what it was like to be utterly poor. Then, talk to her about your heart. How do you feel about your interior poverty? How does your financial situation affect your ability to be spiritually poor? If you are struggling financially, what is your attitude towards it? If you are not struggling, what is your attitude toward what it takes to be financially secure?

For Your Prayer

Mary would have prayed with the book of Zephaniah. Prepare your imaginative prayer by reading Zephaniah 2 and 3. Use your spiritual senses and imaginatively pray with Mary in Luke 2:6. Then, pray this prayer:

"Father, I ask for the grace today to taste your strength in my weakness. I beg you to open my heart so that I embrace my poverty."

What words stood out to you as you prayed?
What did you find stirring in your heart?

_____

_____

_____

_____

_____

_____

_____

_____

_____

_____

_____

_____

_____

_____

_____

_____

_____

_____

_____

_____

_____

DEPENDENT

"Our eyes look to
the LORD."

—Psalm 123:2

AS MARY AND JOSEPH

arrive in Bethlehem, we can take great interest in what is not said about their arrival. Mary and Joseph are returning to Bethlehem, the ancestral home of Joseph's family—yet there is no mention of his family. There is no mention of a relative, no mention of a family caravan, no mention of his plans to reunite with kinfolk.

Imagine what must have been going through Mary's heart. As Mary neared delivery, she was completely dependent upon Joseph as he led her. Joseph led them into Bethlehem, and she knew he had no idea of what they would do when they arrived. Bethlehem's inhospitable welcome of them intensified their dependency on God. They were both utterly dependent on God.

Most of us don't like to be dependent. In fact, our culture champions those who are independent and who go out and make it on their own. However, God has designed us to be dependent because it is there that we most need him.

Where are you most dependent on God? What circumstances in your life are out of your control? What situations will you face this holiday season that will make you feel utterly dependent on God? Where do you feel weak, helpless, or vulnerable?

Now say, "I can't" ... "You can" ... "You promised." That's a great prayer. "God, I can't, but I know you can ... because you promised." Whenever you feel dependent and God is the only one to whom you can turn, say this prayer: "I can't, you can, and you promised." Then, wait with Mary and watch for God to act.

For Your Prayer

Mary would have prayed with the book of Genesis. Prepare your imaginative prayer by slowly reading Genesis 15:1-6; 16:1-16; 22:1-7. Use your spiritual senses and imaginatively pray with Mary in Luke 2:6. Then, pray this prayer:

"Father, I yearn to taste your desire, fidelity, and consistency. I beg you to open my heart so that I embrace dependency."

What words stood out to you as you prayed?
What did you find stirring in your heart?

_____

_____

_____

_____

_____

_____

_____

_____

_____

_____

_____

_____

_____

_____

_____

_____

_____

_____

_____

_____

SIMPLICITY

"In a manger."

—Luke 2:7

SINCE "THERE WAS

no place for them" (Luke 2:7), Mary and Joseph were led to the poorest of places—a manger where animals fed. A tradition of the second century AD places the birth of Christ in a cave on the outskirts of Bethlehem. This tradition was so widespread that around the year 325, the emperor Constantine erected a basilica on this spot to honor the place where Jesus was born.

Scripture and tradition tell us that the place of Christ's birth was simple. No hospital. No physician. No bed. Nothing. Just bare simplicity, among the animals. How fitting. With Mary lying on the naked earth, there was a sweet music that sang to her.

Listen to what we have heard from Mary during Advent: Everything. Nothing. Poverty. Dependence. Emptiness. Echo.

These had been her companions since the Annunciation, and these were her companions as she prepared to give birth to the Messiah. It was a symphony of emptiness, and the orchestra was led by simplicity.

If we embrace Mary, we must embrace simplicity.

Our life can seem awfully busy. The faster our frenzied life becomes, the more complicated it feels. Being overly busy cramps our spirit. Life gets complicated, and the simplicity of God's design grows crowded. On the other hand, with simplicity we have nothing—nothing else except God. There, we are completely receptive to the glory of God, deep union, and our soul's deepest desire. It is pretty simple—simplicity leads us to God.

Ask Mary to reveal the utter simplicity of "the manger." Ask her to help you really focus on Christmas, on its true meaning.

So, we end where we began. Slow down. Get quiet. Listen. After all, what is the rush? What are we really preparing for?

For Your Prayer

Mary would have prayed with Psalm 131. Prepare your imaginative prayer by slowly reading Psalm 131. Use your spiritual senses and imaginatively pray with Mary in Luke 2:7. Then, pray this prayer:

"Father, I ask for the grace today to slow down. Prepare my heart so that I might experience miracles this Christmas."

What words stood out to you as you prayed?
What did you find stirring in your heart?

_____

_____

_____

_____

_____

_____

_____

_____

_____

_____

_____

_____

_____

_____

_____

_____

_____

_____

_____

The Fourth Week of Advent

Bethlehem

RECOLLECT

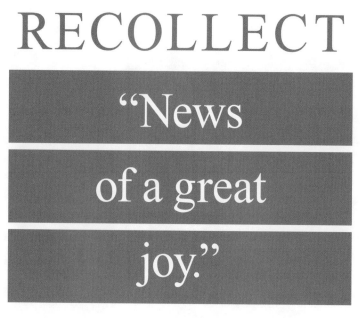

"News of a great joy."

—Luke 2:10

AS WE FIND OURSELVES

actively entering into the fourth week of Advent, we are invited during these days to begin intentional preparation for Christmas. How we prepare in these days depends on what we are preparing for. In other words, there is a difference between preparing for a day versus preparing for a person.

There is a temptation in the days immediately preceding Christmas to focus on December 25. There are lots of details to be tended to: Where are we going to be for the holidays? Are we hosting or are we visiting? What are we bringing or what are we preparing? Are there last-minute gifts to buy? Do we have everything we need? Has everyone's name been checked off the list? There is much to do and many details that require our attention in preparation for Christmas day.

Those details are important. God wants us to celebrate the gift of the Holy Family within the community of our own families. The Incarnation reminds us that God is a part of life, our human experience. However, Mary was not preparing for a day; she was preparing for a person. In the days immediately preceding the very first Christmas, the Mother of God was focused on the person who was to be born. Because her focus was on a person, her preparation was not lost in the details of the day but in her being ready for the person on whom the day was going to center itself.

Imagine for a moment what would have been in Mary's heart as she anticipated the birth of her son. Imagine how many times she sang to Jesus while he was in her womb.

Imagine how many times the child within her would have stirred in her womb as she began to sing to him. Imagine Mary's anticipation of giving birth to the Savior of the world. Imagine what these days of preparation can be for you if you prepare with Mary and like Mary.

The best way for us to prepare for a person is to prepare with a person. In these final days preceding Christmas we invite you to pray with Mary in two very specific ways.

Recall

First, review this journal with Mary. Look back on the meditations that were most personal to you. Returning to the meditations that may have stirred much within you allows you to deepen a conversation with God, who was speaking to you through your meditations. The written text in this journal was intended as a way for you to hear God speaking to you. Those conversations may have more to say if you return to the places in your heart where God was speaking to you. The first way you can prepare for the person is to return to the meditations where the Author of Christmas was speaking to you.

Make Space

The second way you can prepare for Christmas is to make space in your heart for Christ. Mary was empty of anything that would prevent her from receiving God. Likewise, we should be empty of anything that would prevent us from receiving Christ this Christmas. To empty our heart to receive Jesus at the very beginning of his life, we should follow the commands that Jesus himself gave us at the end of his life. In the twentieth chapter of John's Gospel, Jesus reveals himself to the apostles after his resurrection. There, in the upper room, he asks them to receive the Holy Spirit, thereby empowering them to act on his behalf. Jesus gives his apostles, and every bishop and priest going forward, the power to forgive sins on his behalf. He does so because he longs for us to live in freedom. He does so because he wants you to live in freedom. Imagine walking into this Christmas with a heart that is free. If we want to prepare for a person, the best thing we can do is celebrate the sacrament of reconciliation prior to Christmas.

An invitation to go to confession may elicit a variety of emotions in you. Perhaps it has been a long time since you have been to confession. Perhaps there are things in your life now that you would feel vulnerable admitting in the sacrament. Perhaps there are sins from your past that you failed to confess because of a fear of what the priest would think. These feelings are normal. These reservations are understood. The good news is that God wants your freedom more than anything that we just mentioned. All you need to do is take a step forward, and God will do the rest. You have a choice presented to you this Advent. Either you can live the rest of your life with those things preventing you from being free, or you can take this opportunity to finally let them go. Doing so allows you to live the rest of your life with a heart that is free to receive all that God has in store for you.

The truth is that God wants to give you a gift this Christmas. At a time when we may be busy getting gifts for others, God wants to give you the gift of himself. Are you ready to receive his gift? Are you free to receive his gift? Can you trust him this year to receive all that he wants to give you? The only thing that can happen if you celebrate the sacrament of reconciliation is your freedom. Now is the time. Go to confession before Christmas.

For Your Prayer

Mary would have prayed with the Psalms. Choose any of the prompts you have prayed with this Advent. Prepare your imaginative prayer by slowly reading the Psalm. Use your spiritual senses and imaginatively pray with Mary in the Scripture. Then, pray this prayer:

"Father, I ask for the grace today to recollect what you have shown me this Advent. Prepare my heart to receive Christ this Christmas more fully than I ever have before."

What words stood out to you as you prayed?
What did you find stirring in your heart?

_____

_____

_____

_____

_____

_____

_____

_____

_____

_____

_____

_____

_____

_____

_____

_____

_____

_____

_____

What's Next?

Visit **rejoiceprogram.com** for more information
on any of these great follow-ups to *Rejoice!*

ASCENSIONPRESENTS

Ascension Presents is your home for free Catholic media to keep you going throughout the week. Find videos, podcasts, and blog posts from people like Fr. Josh Johnson, Fr. Mike Schmitz, Danielle Bean, Jeff Cavins, and many others!

DON'T WALK ALONE

Following Jesus can be difficult, especially in today's world, and it is especially difficult in isolation. For many years, author and speaker Michael Gormley has been helping people come together, form groups, and grow in friendship with each other and Christ. **Don't Walk Alone** is the first in a series of programs designed specifically to build Christ-centered friendships and groups. Get two or three people together, download the free videos and discussion questions, and start having meaningful conversations—together.

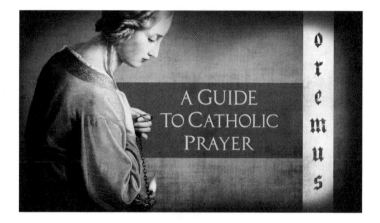

OREMUS

We all desire an intimate relationship with God. But, since learning to "say our prayers" as children, many of us never moved beyond rote recitation to an authentic conversation with God. For most of us, prayer becomes a source of frustration as we struggle to calm our minds and find even a few minutes to set aside to pray. The good news is you can overcome your difficulties with prayer, and it is easier than you might think. *Oremus,* led by Fr. Mark Toups, teaches you the essentials of an effective and fruitful prayer life. Over the course of eight weeks you will discover how God speaks to you, even in the smallest encounters.

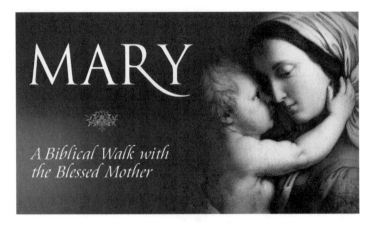

MARY: A BIBLICAL WALK WITH THE BLESSED MOTHER

You've walked with Mary through Advent. Now you can take an extraordinary pilgrimage to find Mary's unique role in God's kingdom and in our lives. Featuring Dr. Edward Sri and filmed on location in the Holy Land, *Mary: A Biblical Walk with the Blessed Mother* will place you in the midst of the powerful drama of Mary's earthly life, taking you through her joys and her sorrows. You will continue to learn how Mary works in our lives today and draws us ever closer to her divine Son. Mary will become a part of your daily life, and in your daily life, you will become more like Christ.